Dreams & Disasters

By Don Adamson

Published by Don Adamson
PO Box 651, Vandalia, OH 45377
www.acts29missions.org

ISBN 978-0-9964824-4-8

Edited by Kathy Kinzig

Dedication

This book is dedicated to all the Haitian missionaries
that sacrifice so much in one of the most difficult
nations of the world. Your labors are not in vain.

*"He will not falter or be discouraged till he establishes
justice on earth. In His teaching the islands will put their
hope." Isaiah 42:4*

The Dream

Come with me on a journey…a journey that covers time and space. I trust that by the time you reach the end of this book, you will find yourself part of the destination. Our journey propels us forward; to step out, putting one foot in front of the other. The steps will be agonizing, yet exhilarating. Join me as we embark on an expedition using Mark 10:29-31 as our guidepost. The scripture reads:

"Truly I tell you," Jesus replied, "no one who has left home or brothers or sisters or mother or father or children or fields for me and the gospel will fail to receive a hundred times as much in this present age…"

Mark 10:29

The farther we drove, the hotter I could feel my face get as my blood pressure began to rise. As our Honda all-terrain vehicle was trudging through the mud, the thoughts that raced through my mind were, *"why are we going this way?"* If this was a joke, I sure wasn't laughing.

My Haitian Director, Jean Bernard, had been in search of property in the city of Cabaret for the last few months. All our Haitian staff agreed that we needed to find a place that was easier to reach and to do ministry from. It wasn't that the base camp we built in Ropissa Village wasn't working; in fact, it was quite the opposite. We are experiencing many successful programs there. The problem was that the road to reach it was breaking our trucks, motorcycles and even us due to the remote location. When we built the base camp in 2011, we had access to a lower road that ran alongside the river. But, that lower road washed away from a tropical storm in 2016. This loss left us with only one way to reach the property in Ropissa village, which was the high road that went over the top of the mountain. It is a bone-crushing ride as we are always fighting rocks, mudslides and deep holes. After a heavy rain, which occurs almost every night in rainy season, the road changes. Where we once had a somewhat smooth gravel surface, we suddenly had huge holes from the water rushing down the mountain into the Caribbean. (*Go to www.dreamsanddisasters.org to see the picture*)

I explained to Jean Bernard that in his search for property in Cabaret, I didn't need much as far as comfort. I just needed a piece of property that was closer to the highway to give us easier access to do ministry without damaging our vehicles so much. A parcel where we could park our vehicles at night, a close water source and security so our American guests would feel comfortable when they visit us. Other than that, I really didn't care what, or where the property was located.

After landing in Port-Au-Prince that day, Jean Bernard said he wanted to show me some land in Cabaret. To my surprise, he took me to the top of a hill that I knew all too well. You see, in 2001 I stood on this very hill and asked God to give our ministry this very land. Back then, I anointed the land with oil and prayed over the north, south, east and west of that hillside. I even took a dollar bill and ripped it in half. Half of it was placed under a rock on the property; the other half is in my bible to this day. I told God that this was my dream and that the ground below my feet was my dream property. From that hillside, I would dedicate myself to evangelizing the nation of Haiti to complete, not just my dream, but His dream, which is to bring people to Him.

As Jean Bernard stopped the engine of our Honda and stepped off, I closed my eyes as the memories from 2001 quickly came back. I could hear the noise of the wind and the smell of the city, just as I remembered it. Jean Bernard broke the silence by asking me what I thought. My tranquility of memories quickly ended as I could feel my blood pressure continuing to rise, and I looked over at him and simply said, "This isn't funny." To which he looked at my expression trying to figure out what I was saying.

"You know what this hillside means to me," I said. "This was my dream to be on this hill over 16 years ago, but you know how that all ended in such painful disaster. I don't think this is funny that you brought me up here." *(Read "The Jesus of My Agony", published in 2016)*

As Jean Bernard began speaking, clarity returned to me as he explained away my confusion. He reminded me that he wasn't with me 16 years ago. We were just acquaintances back then because he worked for another missionary. Although he heard of me, I had another Haitian helping in 2001. He was just a young man when I stood on that hill many years ago. So that day he drove me up to that hillside, he genuinely was on a quest to find the property that met my requirements. As a matter of fact, there was a new owner of the land from when I was wanting it. He wasn't even talking to the same people that I was when I so desired that property. There wasn't any memory for him of that property or what that land meant to me. (*Go to www.dreamsanddisasters.org to see the picture*)

With that knowledge, let's revisit that scripture in the gospel of Mark.

*"Truly I tell you," Jesus replied, "no one who has left home or brothers or sisters or mother or father or children or fields for me and the gospel will fail to receive a hundred times as much **in this present age: homes, brothers, sisters, mothers, children and fields..."***

Mark 10:29-30 continued

Could it be true? Could the dream still be alive in heaven, even though it had long slipped through my fingers here on earth? I felt like a photo album in my brain opened as I looked at the towering mountains to the north. As I spun around, the beautiful white-tipped waves of the Caribbean waters were to the south. As it was late in the day, I could see the sun setting over the shoreline to the west and city lights appearing in Port-Au-Prince to the east. It was exactly as I remembered it. Nothing had changed, except for the several houses that now stood between the coast and me.

I couldn't help but feel overwhelmed as I thought about all the progress that had transpired with Acts 29 Missions since I last stood on that hill in 2001. This instantly brought back so many memories of how God moved us away from that relatively safe area in Cabaret to the perilous mountains above us. With so many natural disasters hitting Haiti, it was as if God picked us up from the city and dropped us in this remote landscape where the people had no access to any organizations to help them.

As we only had a few staff back then, our entire ministry sat on four wheels. We ministered from one corner of the valley to the other from the back of a pickup truck. It was easy to see that God had His hand on our work. This favor gave us a new vision to look for property that we could center the ministry, although it seemed like we were in the middle of nowhere. As we kept our eyes open, we always noticed this piece of land near a village called Ropissa that seemed to be a perfect fit for the needs of the villages.

That land of just gravel and dirt looked worthless, as it was quite remote. But to me, that rough patch that was perched above the village of Ropissa was holy ground. As I would walk that property long before we had boundaries or a fence, I could feel the presence of God. The very first place I would take visiting teams would be to that area to pray. It was full of thorn bushes, rocks and tarantulas to the naked eye. To God, though, I believe He saw what our tomorrows would look like there. A tomorrow where every person who came onto that land had his or her life changed…a tomorrow where children who could never have an education, could now have one of the best in the nation…a tomorrow where the forgotten could find relief and hope…a tomorrow where the blessing of God could be experienced in every outreach. We knew that this remote tract of land was the property that God was giving us. Oh, but at what a cost!

To see the abundant progress now, the difficulties of working to do something that far back in the mountains are a distant memory. It was those difficult times, though, that propelled us to press farther and harder than we ever have before...difficulties that would test our resolve at every turn...literally.

Let us continue through Mark 10:

> *"Truly I tell you," Jesus replied, "no one who has left home or brothers or sisters or mother or father or children or fields for me and the gospel will fail to receive a hundred times as much in this present age: homes, brothers, sisters, mothers, children and fields—along with persecutions..."*

> *Mark 10:29-30 continued*

Let me go down the checklist: Left home-check, left brothers and sisters-check, left mothers and fathers-check, left fields or lands-check. It seems like I qualify for that 100-fold return; but then we come to that next part. The part I wish I could take an eraser and remove from the scripture--"along with persecutions". Say what? How can such a wonderful 100-fold promise of God have those three little words inserted into it? Why couldn't the Lord just pour out my blessing without the persecutions part? Why couldn't I just collect my blessing of that dream property I wanted in Cabaret without the vexations of what we had to endure with the property in Ropissa Village?

Free Property-That Came With A Cost

Backing up several years ago to the year 2011, everything started off great. After years of doing ministry under the shade trees along the riverbank, everyone felt it was time to take a bigger step--not just in ministry, but also in faith.

Following several meetings with the village, there was an agreement that the biggest need of the entire area was a school. As we looked to our vision of "Haitians Changing Haiti", I searched for a partnership which met the needs of the village, with that which Acts 29 could supply. Finally, our staff came up with an agreement that was in sync with the people of Ropissa village. The families would supply the piece of property that we wanted, if I would supply their children a school. The papers were drawn up, boundaries marked off and fund raising planned. After the property was excavated, a strong concrete foundation was poured that the building would be built upon. Everything seemed to be in place and we were just waiting for the delivery of two 40-foot containers that held all the construction pieces of the building. (*Go to www.dreamsanddisasters.org to see the picture*)

During that time of waiting, we were on top of the world, literally. The mountains behind us jut straight up into the clouds from the warm Caribbean waters. The view was breathtaking as we reached the top. As we anticipated the time for the containers to be delivered, we did what we do best--ministry. With over a dozen villages in our care, teams from the United States came to help. One of those teams came from three parts of the United States. The leadership was from Nashville, with all the rest from Houston and Albuquerque. Although all of them would be knocked around the back of my pick-up truck for hours, these were missions-minded people that never complained. That was about to be tested.

While ministering in a village on the very fringe of cell phone reception, I got a call from the shipping company in Port-Au-Prince telling me that our two containers were off the ship and ready to be released from port. Inside each of these containers were 40,000 lbs. of iron, wood and sheet metal that would be assembled to make our school building. In Haiti, they don't give you much grace because there is an expensive fee for every day you keep the containers in storage at the port. So right in the middle of our plans, chaos enters.

The Disaster(s)

I wish the saying "what doesn't kill you can only make you stronger" was never spoken. This was the theme over the next three days for us. We knew our destiny was to have this school in the mountains of Haiti. We had an agreement with elders of the village of Ropissa. Our Board of Directors was excited. Intercessors were organized to pray. Even the finances came through in miracle fashion. God certainly gave us more than our expectations, as the building would be second-to-none in the country. Right in the middle of what we knew was our destiny, though; we learned the hard way that it would come with a cost--a three-day painful cost. We have a saying we use back in those mountains-- "Survive or surrender." Little did we know that saying was about to be put to the test.

We drove back down the mountain that very morning to get to the city where we could plan to receive the containers. On the way down, we received some bad news that the port officials had picked out two trucks for bringing the containers to us. We knew there were some seriously decrepit trucks in Haiti whose lives would have been retired many years ago if these trucks were in the USA. We were hoping that we could pick the trucks and drivers. That bad news, however, was tempered by our finding a crane right away to go to the property and lift the containers off the trucks. We drove to Port-Au-Prince and pulled into the storage yard of a heavy equipment company. There, sitting right in front of us, was this big beautiful heavy-duty crane being filled with diesel fuel. Things were looking great as we went inside to pay for the rental. I should have known trouble was coming since nothing is ever that easy in Haiti, but everything seemed to be going better than planned. The trucks were on their way, and soon the crane would be heading to our property. If all went well, we would have our containers sitting on the ground by nightfall. I felt so good that I decided to check in with our visiting team of Americans to be sure all was well with them.

Do I need to mention the title to this section is, "The Disasters"? Because as soon as I put eyes on the truck carrying the visiting team, the calamity began. I quickly learned the team was ahead of schedule and their ministry completed as we met them on the road. But, one look at the front of the truck and I could see the front tire was completely flat. The driver didn't notice it as the road was so bumpy.

Flat tire #1

I pulled out our air pump and began filling the tire. I then brought everyone together to lay out our next objectives. Our plan was for me to meet the containers on the highway while sending the team to the hotel for the evening. After a few hugs and high-fives, we were all on our way. I then looked back at our truck and saw that we, too, had a flat tire.

Flat tire #2

After putting air in both trucks, everyone was content as we headed back down towards the highway. Once we entered the asphalt, we came upon one of our semi-trucks on the side of the road. We quickly learned that they had three flat tires as the weight of the containers just burned them up.

Flat tires #3, 4 and 5

I was discouraged that the hydraulics in their jack was much like their tires…not in good shape. But, luckily, I had a new 10-ton jack that I just so happened to purchase a couple days before. As I watched, I was shocked to see them jack up the semi-truck bed, take off the flat tires, only to be replaced by some of the tires that were still holding air in the front of the truck. They were not jacking the truck up to fix or replace the tires; they were just shuffling the flat tires around, so they had at least one good tire on each axle. I counted eight good tires being bolted next to eight flat ones. This is Haiti, though, and I just assumed these guys had been doing this for as long as they have been driving trucks. *(Go to www.dreamsanddisasters.org to see the picture)*

With my arms crossed, I stood and watched them in astonishment. Suddenly, someone who knew us and had knowledge that we had two containers coming, called to us and said the second truck made a wrong turn down the road that went along the river. Indeed, that road would take you to our property in Ropissa, but it was barely passable in my heavy-duty four-wheel drive truck. There was no way that a semi-truck would make it; and if we didn't get to them soon, they would reach the point in the road where it would be impossible to turn around. Therefore, I called my driver that was on our Kawasaki all-terrain vehicle and told him to quickly rush down the river road and stop the truck before it was too late. I felt good as we probably averted a crisis, as the ATV raced down that bumpy road in a dust storm. It only made it a mile or so before it, too, had a flat tire.

Flat tire #6

After using one of our small air pumps that we could plug into a cigarette lighter, the tire had enough air for them to continue to catch the semi-truck; but to their surprise, they didn't have to go far as the truck was sitting stopped in the middle of the road with two flat tires.

Flat tires #7 and 8

Believe it or not, they used that cheap little air pump that we used just for our small ATV and motorcycle tires to give it just enough air to turn the truck around. That, in itself, was two miracles as the tires were under such a heavy load and there was barely enough room to turn around without falling into the river.

As we continued to be amazed how the driver of the first semi-truck was doing musical chairs with his tires on the side of the road, the second finally pulled out onto the highway from the wrong road he had taken. He parked behind the first truck and was asking the driver to take two tires off his truck to replace the two that were barely holding air on his own. A big argument erupted as they fought over who should get the better tires. When I say "better" tires, that is a huge stretch. Some of the tires that were holding air had the steel belts sticking out of them because the tread had worn off a long time ago. It was obvious someone was going to have to go buy a couple tires. If I wanted these containers on my property, that someone was going to be me.

I sent one of my staff to go to the tire repair shops on the side of the road and try to find a couple used truck tires. During all this confusion and arguing we heard this large truck passing us. You guessed it...it was the crane. We flagged him down and explained that we are waiting for tires. He knew the roads were going to be difficult and his trek back to our area slow. I sent one of my staff with him and off they went to be ready for us when we arrived.

After what seemed like hours, we finally had at least one good tire on each corner of the bed. Some of the flat tires bolted to the truck were so dilapidated that they just flopped around as useless pieces of rubber, but at least we were ready to make progress. (*Go to www.dreamsanddisasters.org to see the picture*)

We reached the mountain road and began our assent. Black smoke billowed out of the trucks as the engines were feeling the strain of so much weight. Once we came around the first turn, we had to immediately stop, as the crane that should have already been on the property was right in front of us blocking the road. You can imagine what my first response was. "Do we have a flat tire?"

I should have known it was going to be grave as everyone just stared at me with blank faces. As my inquisition continued, I soon got good news and bad. The good news was that it wasn't a flat tire. This was a huge relief, as the tire size for that big crane would have been difficult, if not impossible to find. Then came the bad news. The engine on that crane didn't have enough power to make it up the hill. I took one look at this humongous machine and thought that they had to be joking. Surely, a piece of equipment that large would have one beefy engine. After a few attempts of hearing this engine roar, the tires didn't budge. I soon realized the engine on the crane was much like the tires on the semi-trucks--worn out! I thought to myself, "we are so stuck", as my hope and the sun that day were both setting.

Although this first hill was the longest, it certainly wasn't the steepest. Even if we could pull this heavy equipment with a truck, there would be no way we could do that on the other hillsides in front of us. All I could do was watch the semi-trucks carefully pass us in the gravel to get the containers to the property, even though we didn't have a crane to lift them. However, all was not lost, as we got the phone number for another crane company. As the sky was getting darker, we arranged for the new crane to join us the next day. I sent the Kawasaki ATV to pick up the two truck drivers and take them to a hotel for the night.

All is well, I thought to myself. We can try this again tomorrow. Then, my phone rang.

The semi-trucks were not at the property as we thought. They had good success on the road with only one more hill to climb, but that last incline was the steepest. Neither truck had enough power to get up that hill.

By the time I got there to see for myself, both trucks were sitting on the side of the road at the bottom of the hill. Once I arrived, the driver of one of the trucks thought that he would show me the problem. After backing up 100 feet or so, he stomped on the gas pedal. With a nuclear cloud of smoke pouring from the tailpipe, he headed straight up the incline. Everything looked good as he was making progress; but as the truck continued its ascent, the weight of 40,000 lbs. began to work against gravity. When you have a dilapidated truck, pulling a heavy load in lots of gravel, gravity always wins. It was only a matter of time when his truck came to a grinding halt. Once again, they were all directing the driver to inch his way back towards bottom of the hill. In the United States we would be able to find fault with these trucks and drivers. But in Haiti, this problem was all mine, meaning, a problem that I alone had to solve as nobody had any resources to help. *(Go to www.dreamsanddisasters.org to see the picture)*

The Devil In The Sky

As frustrating as all of this was, a new problem was appearing. As I looked up into the sky, there was a vortex of angry black clouds that were swirling overhead. In the tropics, sometimes one tropical storm can be more violent than a hurricane. This was one of those times. It doesn't matter what you're doing, when you see these storms appear in the mountains, you stop everything and hunker down. We have a saying that rings so true, "Mountains turn grey, quickly run away!" In what seemed just a matter of minutes, mountain after mountain disappeared behind the grey curtain of rain.

By the time the semi-truck finished his retreat down the hill, a wave of wind and water hit us that felt like a wall of needles. Everyone went running for shelter. The drivers raced to the protection of their truck cabs as the workers ducked under the trailers. The two other Americans and I ran full speed to our truck. Although it was only a couple hundred feet away, we were completely soaked by the time we reached the doors and threw ourselves inside where it was dry. The rain was pouring from the sky so hard that all you could see and hear was a blanket of grey noise all around us. I could only barely make out the image of the rectangle trailers through the haze of the tempest. (*Go to www.dreamsanddisasters.org to see the picture*)

Then, to my amazement, we began to watch the trailers start to rock back and forth. I inched my truck closer to witness them sliding sideways in the mud. With the natural slope of the land, the blasts of wind were literally pushing the trailers off the road! Each gust would rock the trailers to each side as if the tires were walking their way to the cliff and certain destruction. If those trailers went over, we would never be able to pull them back. As soon as I had the thought to get out and try to put big rocks under the wheels, I started counting the seconds between lightning strikes. 1...2...3... CRACK! 1...2...3...CRACK! There was lightning hitting all around us every three seconds. The thunder resonated off the sheet metal roof of my truck like a drum. I was in a war of conflicting emotions. With all my thoughts running as fast as the lighting cracking around me, I felt powerless to do anything about it. It was as if I was watching a horror movie and couldn't pull the plug to turn it off. But, in the heat of this battle, I still had one more trick up my sleeve.

My idea was to position my 4-wheel drive truck between the corner of the trailer and the edge of the road. From there I could push against it to keep it from sliding off the mountainside. Just as I started to make my move, though, the storm ended as quickly as it had begun, which is typical in the tropics. Within several minutes, the purple and orange rays of the Caribbean sunset were pushing through the holes in the clouds and the moon and stars appeared above us. Flashes of lighting went off in the distance as the storm headed out to sea. In the yellow rain that was still sprinkling around us, we all came out of hiding. "What was *that*?" one of the Americans asked. "I think that is what we call a devil," I said as I went into cleanup mode. "I have never seen anything like that!" he exclaimed. Even though we were all wet and muddy, everyone was safe. The containers were stuck at the bottom of the hill, and there was nothing we could do about it that night. I brought our security guard from our property to stand guard over the containers as we took the drivers to sleep at a local hotel.

I can't remember if I enjoyed that night of sleep or not. What I do know is that it would be the last night I could sleep for the next 48 hours. After a nice breakfast with the American team the next morning, we all headed for the truck with the goal of seeing the containers reach our property. When we got to the parking lot, there sat the ominous sign of a flat tire looking at us as if to prophesy what kind of day we are about to have.

<u>Flat tire #9</u>

After airing up the tire, we were on our way. I called a good friend of ours in Port-Au-Prince who had a backhoe. I explained the situation and was so blessed that he stopped his construction work and sent one of his guys up the mountain to clear out some of the gravel that kept prohibiting our semi-trucks making it up the hill. Once that process was underway, I went to get my money back on the first crane that couldn't make it and go pay for the second crane. To my dismay, they didn't want to give the money back because the owner of the crane was saying the problem was the road, not his crane. Frustration set in as I explained if that were the case, he wouldn't be able to do anything in Haiti as most all the roads are in bad shape. After some aggravating conversations, he agreed to give me back a portion.

With partial money back and a new connection for the second crane, we called the crane operator and agreed to meet him to pay for the rental. We would trust that he would come out quickly and get the containers unloaded. After taking care of business, we rushed back to the mountain to see what progress was made with the semi-trucks.

As I ascended the mountain, the first thing I saw as I came around corner was becoming a familiar sight. One of the trucks jacked up with two flat tires.

Flat tires #10 & 11

Because there were no more extra inflated tires to make a swap with, we once again found ourselves running around the city trying to find a truck tire. As we negotiated with one of the tire repair places on the side of the road, the owner sent a young man to a house across the street. Out of the front door came a good tire that would work. I had to think how weird it was that the man was living with all the good tires in his house. When we agreed on a price, the driver informed me he had no money and couldn't pay for the tire. I think he realized that he was stuck, which in reality meant, I was stuck. So, once I paid for the new tire and repair of the second one, off we went back up the mountain.

We were met by progress as the truck that had enough inflated tires to go forward was about to try again to go up the hill. This time the road had been cleared of loose gravel and the backhoe was pushing the truck from behind. With both machines bellowing black smoke, the truck began making its way up the hill. I wish I could say how exhilarating it was to watch the truck slowly disappear up the hill and around the corner, but the reality was we had another truck with flat tires to deal with.

The day seemed to go quick as the hint of late afternoon sun was giving into dark clouds once again. I was feeling good with the prospect of getting the trucks to the property just as my phone rang. It was one of my staff telling me that the crane had a mechanical problem and wouldn't be able to reach us that day. In the mission field, oftentimes you must take what you can get. So, just as the backhoe was coming back to us after pushing the first truck up the hill, we were lowering the two jacks after changing the tires. If I could just get both trucks to the property before dark, even a foot at a time, I would call that a success. (*Go to www.dreamsanddisasters.org to see the picture*)

The first small drops of rain had just begun hitting us when we finally were able to park both trucks side-by-side on the property. After giving instructions to our security guard, we quickly loaded up and got back down the mountain before the big rains came. Once we reached the bottom, our staff turned left to take the two drivers back to the local hotel, as I turned right to get the American team back to their hotel. The black clouds looked like they wanted to flow right down the mountain range and sweep us into the ocean, but time was on my side as I had a few minutes jump on the storm…or so I thought. Halfway to the hotel I could hear a high-pitched hissing sound. Before I could pull over to investigate, the vibration of the truck quickly told me what the problems was. Flap…Flap…Flap… could be heard as our blown-out tire was flopping all over the road.

Flat tire #12

I felt that we were all getting into the rhythm of NASCAR pit crew status, as we had been changing tires for two days. Some of them we could just put air into and keep going since the leaks were small, but one look at my shredded tire told me that a little air wouldn't help us this time. We unloaded the American team from the back of the truck and started jacking it up. I was thankful that our staff had enough wisdom to get my second spare tire repaired at the same time we were dealing with the semi-truck tires. We were changing the tire in record time, but certainly not fast enough to keep us dry as the storm hit us with high winds and heavy rain. There wasn't enough room in the front of the truck to hold everyone, so there was no other option but to reload everyone in the back and cover them with a tarp.

We must have been a sight as we all unloaded at the hotel and headed for dinner. Because we were late, there wasn't time for everyone to change clothes. So here we were, this rag-tag group of cold, muddy and wet Americans dragging into the cafeteria. After I parked the truck, I began to rehearse in my mind my apologies for such a stressful day. After all, they came to be on a mission's trip, not a transportation charade. To my surprise, everyone was happy and joking about the day.

I felt such a relief of pressure as each one had a different story to tell from the same day we all experienced. As they waited for trucks to show up, some of them went into the villages to pray for people, others did a Kids Club for the children around our property and still others did a Widows Care program. I was grateful the team took charge of these events since I had my hands full trying to get the containers up the mountain. It ended up being a great night of fellowship and worship as the tropical rain was pouring down all around us.

When we were done, I went back to my room to take an inventory of what finances I had left. Because of all the commotion, there was no time to be thrifty. Money was pouring from my pockets about as fast as the rain was falling from the sky. As I watched my wife snuggle under the blankets, I plugged into the hotels internet service and began shooting out emails requesting financial help to just about everyone I knew. I wondered if anyone would believe me in telling them we had 12 flat tires in 2 days. (*Go to www.dreamsanddisasters.org to see the picture*)

As I finished the last email, I could see just a little glimmer of sunshine coming over the mountains. Day two was over and day three was coming at us fast. Could it be that we could get everything done in the morning since it seemed most everything is in place? We just needed that crane to get up the mountain and unload the containers off the semi-truck beds.

After we met the staff and the drivers in the city, we all gathered up the supplies we would need for the day and headed back up the mountain. Even though I had our 4-wheel drive truck loaded with people, I was surprised how just how treacherous the muddy road was. It seemed that the storm that was dumping so much rain yesterday stayed around for quite a while that night. Everywhere we went we saw damage the villages took during the storm.

This was most evident as we were only a few hundred yards from our property, and one of the houses that was built on the side of a hill was torn apart. We met the woman who owned the house holding everything she possessed in two pillowcases. The storm took the rest. With the promise of our return to help her, we continued around the corner to see the damage to our property. My first scan of the property told me just how strong the storm was. "Where is our water tower?" I asked the bewildered guard. To our astonishment our water tower had been completely blown over into one of our metal storage buildings. There was 200+ gallons of water weighing down a tower made of iron. To this day, we continue to be amazed at the power of the wind. (*Go to www.dreamsanddisasters.org to see the picture*)

A plan was quickly made as half the American team went to get supplies to fix the woman's washed out house and the others stayed behind to get the water tower out of the building and standing straight up again. The good news was that the backhoe was still on our property. We could use a couple towing chains to connect the tower to the boom arm of the backhoe. Slowly we could pull the tower up and back onto the foundation. A sense of relief came when we saw the water tank was not damaged, and we were able to place it back on top of the tower. As you have probably come to expect, though, relief in this environment never lasts long.

After a couple hours of working with the water tower, our other truck pulled into the property covered in mud and loaded with the building supplies to fix the broken house. Our driver got out to tell us the bad news of the crane stuck in the mud halfway down the mountain. I knew it was a struggle just to get our 4-wheel drive through the mud, so it wasn't such shocking news that the crane was stuck. We still had the backhoe with us, though, and we were just finishing the repairs to the water tower. After putting some fuel in the backhoe and unloading the building supplies, they both drove away to rescue our crane.

After a couple hours, I got the call that the crane was free. "*Finally*," I thought. "*It can continue its journey to our property.*"

But before I could end the call, the driver spoke up and said, "That was the good news."

When I heard him say that, I braced myself for the bad news. I asked him, half-jokingly, "Does the crane have a flat tire?"

He said, "No, the crane tires are just fine." I felt some relief, but only for a split second as he continued, "The bad news is, the backhoe has a flat tire and is sitting on the side of the mountain."

Flat tire #13

I think that part of me was hoping this was all a joke since we had such bad luck with tires in the last three days. If ever there was such a thing as a "demon of tires" sent from hell, we sure were fighting it. The long pause on the end of the line, though, told me that this was not a joke. Not only did we have a flat tire, but also the driver of the backhoe couldn't spend any more time with us and had to get back to Port-Au-Prince. For the moment, though, we were making progress on the plan of getting the containers off the semi-trucks. As soon as I could be sure the American team was set with everything they needed to fix that broken house, I raced down the mountain to get the backhoe driver to the city and shop for a used tire. After making some phone calls on the way, we found a man who had a used tire of the size that we needed. I couldn't believe my good fortune as we loaded the tire in our truck and called a tire repairman to let him know we would be picking him up as well.

Fast forward a few hours later, and we were putting the final lug nuts on the backhoe. With sweat pouring down my face, it was getting late in the afternoon and I really needed to get to the property to see how they did with getting the containers off the semi-trucks. So, I arranged our truck to return to the city with the tire repair people while I drove the backhoe.

Belief In Our Disbelief

At this point you may not believe all my stories about this many flat tires. I would probably have a hard time believing it myself, but I have more than 20 witnesses who experienced all of this with me. When we heard of another flat tire, we shook our heads in disbelief. The other part of my story that may be hard to believe is how incredibly strong the storms were that hit us each afternoon. During rainy season in the tropics, afternoon thunderstorms happen for many weeks at a time, yet we were all surprised just how strong these storms were. Over the three days, every storm was a major event. I said all of that to set up this next paragraph.

Once we repaired the flat tire on the backhoe, we took one look at the top of the mountain and knew another storm was advancing in strength and would soon be heading our way. It would be impossible to get the backhoe down the mountain to the safety of the city. I decided the best idea was to get it back to our property. The problem was that we no longer had a driver. I have never driven a backhoe in my life, but the setting sun and the storm clouds brewing weren't going to allow me to get an experienced backhoe operator up this mountain. So, I sat inside the cab and learned by trial and error. This bar lifted the front arm, the other one, the back. A couple more moved the stability arms on the side. Then, I finally found the one that moved us ever so slowly forward. I couldn't believe it! In my first experience in driving a backhoe, I was going forward, and all was well. My dream was to pull into the property and see those big red containers on the ground. So, after about 100 yards of jubilation, I heard a large explosion behind me. It only took one glance over my shoulder to see the problem. The used tire we put on the backhoe just 20 minutes before was a bad tire and it had blown out as well.

Flat tire #14

The stress of all of this was reaching my limit. As I stepped out of the backhoe, I could see a hole in the side of the tire as big as my fist. I wasn't sure if it was my tears starting to run down my face or the drops of rain that just started falling from the sky. Either way, I found myself, once again, with a flat tire in a violent tropical storm. I had no other option but to leave the backhoe in the middle of the road and try to get to the relative safety of our property.

I felt like my blood was boiling. It seemed that the more progress we made, the harder it got. We were now on day three and still no containers had touched the ground of our property. I thought things couldn't get worse, but I was wrong.

After we abandoned the backhoe, we came around a corner, there sat our crane on the side of the road. It was raining so hard that the team of men that came with the crane was huddled underneath it trying to stay dry. The sideways rain was going to make sure that didn't happen.

As for me, I just didn't care anymore. I took a big breath, opened my door and walked back to the truck. They looked at me in disbelief, as I seemed oblivious to the pelting rain. I think my anger and frustration simply made me numb to the stinging barrage of water hitting my face. Within only a few seconds, I was soaked as I surveyed all the tires that seemed to be in good shape. I yelled at the men under the crane asking why they stopped and what was wrong. Their response put me over the edge. They said they were out of fuel. What?!? How could they come all this way from the city and not have enough fuel to reach the destination? In just a couple more miles they would be unloading the containers. I asked what they were going to do. They said they would send one of the men down by motorcycle to get some fuel; but he knew, as well as I did, that it was impossible to do in the thunderstorm.

As I mentioned before, my stress level was at its maximum range. I could feel my entire insides shaking as I walked back to my truck completely soaked. All I wanted to do was pick up the American team and get back to the hotel. I no longer cared what was going to happen. My thoughts of just trying to move forward was like a hand rubbing over a rusty pipe. Nothing was processing easily, and I knew I just had to get away from it all.

As I pulled onto the property, I had a couple dozen eyes staring at me from under a tarp that was set up to keep everyone dry. It didn't take much discernment to see their expressions of apprehension. I didn't know what was going on, nor did I care. I jumped out of the truck and told the American team to get their stuff together. We were pulling out and heading back to the hotel with no "ands, ifs or buts".

Just then, one of the Americans came to me, and in one sentence, that included each word of "ands, ifs or buts", explained that I had a big problem as he pointed toward the semi-trucks. As I walked toward the trucks, the drivers both got out to meet me. It was easy to perceive they were angry about something. Through the help of a translator, they demanded to know where the crane was. I told them it was close but out of fuel. They were going to have to go down with my staff and spend the night at a hotel again.

At that point, they began yelling and screaming. They said they were tired of sitting there all day, and they were going to drive back down the mountain and try again later. I told them they were crazy. It took them two days just to get to where they were. We were in the middle of a tropical thunderstorm and they wouldn't make it to the very first hill on their way back down. By then, some of the people from the village started fighting with them, as this was "their" blessing sitting in those containers and they weren't going to allow the men to leave. I then tried a different approach and attempted to calmly rationalize with them to try to soothe everyone's frayed nerves. I again explained that even if the conditions were perfect, they weren't going to make it down that mountain. They would lose their trucks and the containers. Soon, a few Americans jumped in and the quarreling started up all over again. Here we were, 25 people, yelling in two different languages, on the side of a mountain, in a rainstorm, all arguing and fighting. How crazy that must have looked.

I simply had enough that night and threw my hands up into the air and told the American team to load up in the back of the truck. I told the drivers that if they were going to try to get down that mountain, they would do so at their own peril. If they slid off the road, which they most surely would, I was not rescuing them; and they would have to pay for their own damages. Even if they could find a tow truck big enough to help them, that alone would take days; but I didn't care. I was getting my team loaded up as all the Haitians were continuing to yell and argue. My decision was made, and nothing was going to stop me from leaving…or so I thought.

Right in the middle of all this stress and confusion, a sudden silence fell on everyone in the crowd. All our eyes were on a set of headlights coming around the corner. I remember saying aloud, but to myself, *"Who in the world is back here at this time of night?"* Then, as the lights came closer, and the curtain of rain became thinner, everyone stared in shock. It was the crane!

The entire team, from the back of my truck, erupted in cheers as everyone shouted and praised God. I got out with my hands on my hips and thought I would cry. Unknown to me, while all the arguing was taking place, two of my staff got on the ATV and went into the city to buy as many containers of diesel fuel as they could find. It was enough to get the crane started and up to our property. Just when all hell was breaking loose, here came our deliverer in the form of a big old crane. As fast as the team loaded up, they unloaded again to see how this was going to work.

It felt like heaven came to earth as the rain moved off to the west and a warm tropical breeze began blowing over us. Soon the stars and moon seemed so close that we could touch them. Even though the ground was saturated, the crane was able to come along side of the first container, albeit a foot deep into the mud. Everyone was taking pictures and celebrating as the crane arm began lifting the first container off the truck. The celebration was short lived, though, as the weight of the container stopped moving up and the crane started moving down. The weight was just too much for the rain-soaked ground and the crane just sunk under the weight. (*Go to www.dreamsanddisasters.org to see the picture*)

My desperation kicked in as I told the villagers and the team to grab as many rocks as they could find…something that is not too hard in Haiti, to shore up the crane. There was a hole had to be filled for the crane to be stabilized. It was somewhat comical as a little bit of everything was being thrown into that cavity in the mud. Broken plastic chairs, pieces of old plywood, a dead banana tree and rocks of every shape and size. Whatever people could find, they threw into the hole.

I wish I could tell you how I watched, inch by inch, as the containers were lifted off the truck. It would make a wonderful story. I could have recorded all the praises and prayers that happened that night. But one look at my watch made reality set in. I had a big dilemma as it was already two hours past dark, and I still had a large team of Americans that had to get down the mountain and to the hotel. It is never a good idea to try to transverse that precarious mountain road in the dark, let alone drive the 40 minutes on a dangerous highway at night. So, I made the decision to let the Haitians deal with the containers as I told the American team to load up once again in the truck.

I heard a few sighs of relief as everyone knew that soon they would be having a nice dinner on the Caribbean and getting a good night's rest. Of course, it never happens that easily; and certainly not on this day, as I looked down and saw the back tire was completely out of air. So, as quickly as I had them load up for the third time, I had to ask them to get back off the truck, so we could air up the tire. The sighs of relief went to sighs of skepticism that they would ever see their hotel room that night.

Flat Tire #15

I never could find the hole in that tire that night under the lights of five or six cell phones and the treads full of mud; but I almost didn't care. I knew the tire was filled with air, and we would have to take the chance of getting down the mountain. I set the timer on my watch to go off every 10 minutes, so I could stop and look at the tire. Of course, going down rocky roads full of mud is not the best environment for checking for flat tires; but at each stop, the tire looked acceptable, so we continued toward the highway.

It felt good to see the flat pavement, as I think everyone was tired of being tossed around on rocks. Once I pulled out onto the asphalt and the noise from all the mud in the tires being thrown off by our progress lessened, I pulled over to put my eyes on that tire once more. I think everyone was praying that it was holding air, at least enough to get to the hotel. As several people once again turned their phone flashlights to the tire, it was easy to see that our hopes were going to be dashed.

Flat Tire #16

I guess if there was any good news in examining that tire, it was that there wasn't any gaping hole we could see. Being that late at night and with everything we had already been through during the day, I decided I could take the gamble and fill it up, as much as possible with the air pump and take my chances in reaching the hotel. There really wasn't any other option since the spare tire was flat simply because we didn't have enough time to stop at the tire repair place and have it looked at earlier in the day. So, with the rattle of the air compressor, I watched the air gauge reach 40…50…60lbs. of air. Everyone was quiet as we held our breath listening to hear air hissing out of the tire; but once everyone confirmed they couldn't hear any noise, we loaded back up yet again.

What a relief it was to finally reach the hotel. We were already three hours late for dinner, but the hotel staff was still there waiting for us. All the frustrations of the day melted away as we were relieved to get off that mountain and enjoy some good, albeit cold, food. Although everyone was exhausted, there was an excitement in the air, as we knew the containers and crane were on the property.

It was a fast meal for the whole team; and as soon as everyone had their bellies full, they focused on getting to their rooms and enjoying a hot shower and good night's sleep. As I excused myself, I let everyone know I would see them in the morning. I could almost hear the gasps as I told them I had to go back to the property so I could get an update with my own eyes on the progress. Besides, my staff had been working hard for the last few days and they didn't have access to any dinner that night. So, with a little "tip" to the headwaiter, I loaded up two plates of food and headed back out to the truck. There was some relief as the questionable tire looked like it was in good shape, and I didn't have to put air in it. I have to say it was very spooky on those pitch-black roads driving through the middle of the night. Being all by myself at night isn't the safest thing to do, but I knew it had to be done.

My mind was starting to drift off to sleep as I was driving up that bumpy road. Many times, the effects of being tossed around inside the cab of a truck would keep me awake, but this time it seemed to be rocking me to sleep. My heavy eyelids quickly opened when a set of headlights coming down the mountain got bigger and bigger. When I got close enough, I could see it was one of the semi-trucks…UNLOADED! I was so happy that I flagged them down and thanked them for the hard work. It wasn't long before the next set of truck headlights was coming at me. What a relief it was to see those empty trucks and that could only mean one thing, the containers were on the ground of our property!

As the third set of headlights appeared in the distance, I could only assume it was the crane coming down the mountains after the task of unloading the containers. Instead, it was our Kawasaki ATV with my two hungry staff members. Perfect timing as I had two plates heaping with hotel food. What a feast we had eating under the full moon celebrating the victory.

Obviously, it didn't take long for the question to fall out of my mouth, "Where is the crane?" I saw frustration and relief at the same time as they shook their heads.

After unloading both 40,000 lb. containers, the crane was now 4 feet deep into the mud and wasn't going anywhere that night. They were able to send the crane operator and his helpers home since they later brought their Nissan truck for transportation. Everyone was assured that night as we had good security watching over everything. A team of farmers had already begun to dig out all the mud from the tires in hopes that the sun would come out as it usually does that next morning to dry out everything.

None of that mattered at the time, though, as we had already accomplished an incredibly difficult task. With relief that we finally got the job done, we started down the mountain and headed to each of our beds for some much-needed sleep…at least that was the plan.

Coup de Grâce

After a quick prayer of thanks, we proceeded down the mountain road with our bellies and minds satisfied. Just as we began to see the few streetlights in the valley below us, another set of lights appeared, but these lights weren't in the distance, but glaring into our face. As we got closer, we could see our two semi-trucks were stuck in the mud, and one was barely hanging onto the side of the mountain. Then, under the light of the full moon, we could see the Nissan truck over in the ditch that had completely succumbed to the muddy road. I couldn't believe it! All the work to get up that mountain and it was the trip down that brought disaster to these trucks.

After surveying the situation, I felt good that an experienced tow truck driver would be able to get them free and back on their way. After all, this wasn't my problem anymore. The containers were delivered, and the drivers were completely paid, tips and all. I offered to take them down to the city if that would help them. As I waited for their answer, one-by-one they stood in front of me. It didn't take too much moonlight reflecting off their faces to read their minds. I immediately said, "No way!" I was completely exhausted from three days of work, and my wife and the American team were all at the hotel waiting for me to finish this fiasco. Besides, I had the Kia truck. Even in 4-wheel drive, it would break apart attempting to pull a semi-truck up a hill in the mud. As we all stood staring at each other, I asked, "Well…what are you going to do?" One man came forward and, with his hands gesturing, he said, "You are all we have." What?! How could I be so close to victory and now right back in the same mess I started with three days ago; mud, big trucks and bad roads.

At this point, I must give credit to my Haitian staff. They are some of the best men in the nation. They learned in our ministry that to decide whether to serve one another isn't an option for us. They seemed to join in the chorus line of eyeballs that are staring at me. I just shook my head, put my hands on my hips, and told them it was impossible as I surveyed the situation. Not only did I not have my heavy-duty Ford truck, on top of that, I didn't have the chains to pull the trucks. The chains were left on the property after we lifted the water tower from the building. My exclamation of, *"This is not my problem!"* simply echoed empty down the valley floor, because it sure didn't register in anyone's ears.

You could hear the rustling of the wind blowing by us as we had a stalemate of silence. In the back of my mind I reasoned, *"Why am I arguing with them about this?"* I learned that I never win in these situations. So, as I threw my hands into the air, my brain changed gears, as it seems to easily do these days, and I went into hyper leadership mode. To the drivers I said, "OK...You put big rocks behind the wheels to keep them from sliding any further toward the edge." To the workers I said, "Get a tire tool and clear out some of the mud and gravel that is in front of each tire." Then to my staff, "You take the ATV, and run back to our property and retrieve the towing chain we used earlier in the day." Then I told them all I would go down to the city and pull out my Ford truck and, hopefully, we will all meet back here at the same time, ready to try this.

I must tell you, I was quite nervous. The first reason was that it was 3:00 a.m. and I lived in the city. Security in Haiti is always something we must consider. Certainly, at 3:00 am, I would have no help if somebody decided they wanted my truck more than me. Still, even if I could get the truck, I wasn't sure I could pull a semi-truck through the mud up the side of the mountain. That truck has been good to us and has never failed, but this was taking it to the extreme.

Around 45 minutes later, we regrouped back on top of the mountain. The semi-trucks were still sitting in the same place, and they had all the gravel and mud cleared from the tires. I was at least thankful that neither semi-truck joined the Nissan truck in the ditch.

About the time I turned my truck around and backed up to the front bumper of the semi, our ATV came roaring around the corner with my two staff members. As I was looking for a solid part of the frame where I could attach the towing hook, I reached out my arm for them to hand me the towing chain. "What is this I asked?" They said it was what I sent them to get so we could pull the trucks out. "I said towing CHAIN, not towing strap!" A towing chain has no problem with pulling something heavy. The towing strap they brought has a tow rating of 3000 lbs. at best. The truck I was pulling was more than double that, not to mention pulling it through the resistance of mud. I am sure my voice sounded a little squeaky when by faith I asked, "Did you happen to bring the chain also?" You can imagine the dead silence as no answer came forth.

The reality of everyone's sheer exhaustion kicked in, and I didn't care anymore. I told them to hook me up with that strap, and we were going to trust God on this one.

Now, I have to say that twice I've broken these types of towing straps. Both times, it was stretched out like a guitar string only to snap and come right through my rear glass window, both times inches from my head. Can you imagine how painful it was to replace the window once, but then to do it a second time? Now, here we were, stretching a strap to its limits again; but I couldn't fathom sitting on that mountain one minute longer than I needed.

So, I dropped my 4-wheel drive transfer case to low range, pulled my transmission to low gear, said a prayer and eased into the gas pedal. Once I felt the resistance of the weight of the semi-truck, I couldn't get my mind from my two occurrences with towing straps. I sunk down deeper into my seat, as if the wire frame and soft fabric of my seat would do any good against a fiberglass strap coming in through my back window. At least it made me feel better as I winced in anguish of what might happen. Suddenly, I felt movement. Once all four tires of my truck began digging into the gravel of the road, the mud began to give up its hold on the tires of the semi-truck. After all the exhaustion, oh, how I really needed to feel the sense of victory at that exact moment. As I peeked into my rear-view mirror, relief flooded my mind as both the semi-truck and I were slowly inching up the hill. Once I got the first truck to safe distance, we unhooked the strap and repeated the same for the second truck.

When we finally got them on top of the hill, there wasn't a "thank you," or "How can we repay you" or anything. Both trucks started their engines and off they went. I think they were probably just as exhausted as we were. The only people standing on that mountain were me, my two staff members and the crane operators from the Nissan truck. One look at my face and he never even asked the question, as he knew he was too far off the road for any help I could bring him. All we could do was put him on the ATV and give him a ride back into the city.

Wonderful fatigue is a good definition of what I was feeling that early Saturday morning as the sky was just starting to give a hint of the sunshine to come. There were a few people milling around the road when I got back to my house to switch trucks. That made me feel more comfortable as I pulled open the noisy metal gate and parked my Ford truck. I even gave that truck a pat on the hood saying, "Sweetheart, you just pulled two semi-trucks up the mountain in the mud." That brought a smile to my face as I jumped into the Kia truck to head over to the hotel just in time for breakfast.

I was feeling so good that finally we overcame all obstacles and got those two containers up on that mountain. I closed the gate with a sense of great accomplishment. I was finally by myself as my mind did a quick review of everything the team and I had been through the last three days. Now it was as if the 40,000 lbs. of the weight of those containers were lifted off my shoulders. The victory had come, and I wanted to shout it from the rooftops.

But then...flap, flap, flap...

Flat Tire #17

Can Anything Good Come Out of Nazareth?

So many difficulties! So much stress! So much bad! What possible good could ever come from such a story? Before answering that, let us take a quick glance at one verse found in John chapter 1 from a man named Nathanael, who asks the similar question after hearing Jesus came from Nazareth;

> "Can anything good come from Nazareth?"
> Nathanael asked. "Come and see," said Philipp.
> John 1:46

Most of us reading this book right now can attest to just how much good did come from Nazareth. How can Gods' goodness even be measured when He sent His

Son for us? Even though Nazareth may have been a scrappy little village, oh what good came from it.

That "good" has a name. His name is Jesus, and He told us that when we do ministry to the very least, we are doing it unto Him. Somehow, someway, when we feed the poor and the hungry lined up with their baskets for food, He is there, in line as well, waiting for His portion. When our students sit on the school benches, He is sitting there too. When poverty loses its hold and joy breaks out in one of our most remote villages, He is belly laughing with us. We may not see Him, but He is there.

Let me bring the silver lining in the clouds with Philipps' answer to Nathanael's question. "Come and see." Only if you have been to Haiti with me would you understand what is happening on that remote piece of property that was so difficult to reach with those containers. The good that came from the flat tires far outweigh the difficulties we faced. Now, the sounds of children's laughter resonate among the mountain cliffs. Happy and healthy students are getting an education that was never available to them before. The elderly and widowed are receiving sustenance for their existence. Women who have been pressed down by their culture are being empowered. Entire economies of many villages have been strengthened. New crops are growing. Witchcraft beliefs, dispelled. The illiterate, being educated. The hungry are being fed. The naked are receiving clothes. Lives are being saved.

What Was Meant For Harm, God Has Turned For The Good!

It's easy to say God is with us in the good times. But, I can promise you, He is there in the bad as well. When I was on the side of the road trying to discern if it was tears or rain that was flowing down my face in the most stressful of times…He was there too. How do I know? Because of the promise we started this book with:

So Jesus answered and said, "Assuredly, I say to you, there is no one who has left house or brothers or sisters or father or mother or wife or children or lands, for My sake and the gospel's, who shall not receive a hundredfold now in this time—houses and brothers and sisters and mothers and children and lands, with persecutions—and in the age to come, eternal life. But many who are first will be last, and the last first."
Mark 10:29-31

When the pain of those three days hit me, I felt I was at the end of the line and the last person on the mind of God. I questioned if He even knew what I was going through. In reality, though, He was saying in that still small voice, "Hang in there My son, even if you feel you are the *last*, you will very soon be the *first* in seeing me transform my people in a small corner of the world called Haiti, in a forgotten place called Ropissa."

To back this statement up, I must tell you about one event. If a picture could tell a thousand words, this one would tell a million. As I was in my most stressful period of dealing with the loss of our second tire on that backhoe, the American team was at our property. At that exact moment a rainbow appeared. Not just generically in the sky. But it was perfectly centered, from one boundary of our property to the other. Under that rainbow sat both semi-trucks and all the mud. In the midst of my breaking point, it was as if God was letting me know, He hasn't forgotten about me. That somehow, someway, the sufferings…dare I say "persecutions" that Mark 10:30 was taking about, was the springboard for the dream to begin. *(Go to www.dreamsanddisasters.org to see the picture)*

The Dream Continues

I can't continue to talk about dreaming without fast-forwarding, and bringing you back to Cabaret, and the hillside property that was my dream back in 2001. Now, all these years later, I found out that the dream didn't go anywhere. God still had it the whole time. Even though those prayers had long slipped from my mind, they were as fresh to God as if I just prayed them. Today as I stand on that hill, I can excitedly tell you that we now own that land. Once again, just like everything else, God provided the finances to get the Cabaret property in a supernatural way. As my Haitian Director stood on that hill, contemplating all the incredible things we could do from that property, God shows up once again with a huge rainbow and light show in the sky above us. Confirmation once again, that the dream continues. (*Go to www.dreamsanddisasters.org to see the picture*)

The Next Step

Now comes the next step of the dream. Getting the buildings needed to be built on that land. This is where you come into the dream. After reading this book, hopefully, you can see the faithfulness of God to keep His promises--even when times look tough. The possessions that we place value on are the very things we had to let go of to see this work in Haiti come to pass. The relationships I painfully said good-bye to, were the exact things He was going to use to keep His promise of, "he shall *receive a hundredfold now in this time.*"

The new property in Cabaret is ours and the timing is now. He doesn't drop buildings out of the sky; He uses people, His people, to see the dreams of men come to pass. As they come to pass, it all starts to look less and less like a man's dream, and more and more like God's dream.

Would you prayerfully consider helping us to build structures on our property? Our needs are for long and short-term housing, a ministry center, offices, security building, and of course, a garage to fix flat tires.

Time is short, and the needs are now. This will be our year to watch the dream become reality as we build on that property. We need your help to do this. I, or any member of our Board of Directors, would be happy to meet with you to discuss how you can make an impact on this ministry…this work…this dream.

If you are already one of our friends and already know of our integrity and accountability, you can help immediately. You can send a check to Acts 29 Missions, PO BOX 651, Vandalia, OH 45377. If you would like to give electronically, you can do that at www.acts29missions.org/donate. If you have any questions, feel free to contact me at don@acts29missions.org or sandee@acts29missions.org.

I would encourage you to act quickly as the events and funds needed for these events are already being set in place to facilitate the school, expand women's ministry, feed the elderly and to do ministry…not construction. To accomplish this much ministry limits our timing to do any type of building campaign. This makes this book our building campaign. So please, take a moment now to ask God what part you have to play in seeing the dream…His dream…come to pass. I prayerfully look forward to your commitments.